Nutribullet Recipe Book

Easy and Tasty Smoothies, Soups, Juices, and More for a Healthier You

MAGGIE .H. JACOBS

Copyright © 2024 By MAGGIE .H. JACOBS. All rights reserved worldwide.

No part of this book may be reproduced or transmitted in any form or by any means, electronic or mechanical, including photocopying, recording, or by any information storage and retrieval system, without written permission from the publisher, except for the inclusion of brief quotations in a review.

Warning-Disclaimer:

The purpose of this book is to educate and entertain. The author or publisher does not guarantee that anyone following the techniques, suggestions, tips, ideas, or strategies will become successful. The author and publisher shall have neither liability nor responsibility to anyone with respect to any loss or damage caused, or alleged to be caused, directly or indirectly, by the information contained in this book.

This copyright notice and disclaimer apply to the entirety of the book and its contents, whether in print or electronic form, and extend to all future editions or revisions of the book. Unauthorized use or reproduction of this book or its contents is strictly prohibited and may result in legal action.

TABLE OF CONTENT

INTRODUCTION 6
    PURPOSE OF THE BOOK AND TARGET AUDIENCE 7

CHAPTER 1: BREAKFAST BLASTS 9
    Green Smoothie Bowl 9
    Tropical Fruit Parfait 9
    Peanut Butter Banana Protein Shake 10
    Overnight Oats Smoothie 10
    Berry Breakfast Blast 11
    Tropical Green Machine 11
    Cinnamon Roll Smoothie 12
    Carrot Cake Smoothie 13
    Mocha Protein Smoothie 14
    Pumpkin Pie Smoothie 14

CHAPTER 2: ENERGIZING SMOOTHIES 15
    Berry Beet Refresher 15
    Mango Madness 15
    Green Machine 16
    Chocolate Peanut Butter Cup 16
    Citrus Zinger 17
    Blueberry Almond Delight 17
    Kale Pineapple Energizer 18
    Strawberry Banana Blast 18
    Coconut Cashew Crave 19
    Ginger Peach Punch 19

CHAPTER 3: SOUPS AND STEWS 20
    Creamy Tomato Soup 20
    Butternut Squash Bisque 21
    Chilled Gazpacho 22
    Hearty Lentil Stew 23

Broccoli Cheddar Soup 24

Carrot Ginger Soup 25

Black Bean Soup 26

Roasted Red Pepper Soup 27

Sweet Potato Coconut Curry Soup 28

Minestrone Soup 29

CHAPTER 4: SAUCES AND DIPS 30

Guacamole 30

Hummus 31

Salsa 32

Cashew Cheese Sauce 33

Tzatziki Sauce 34

Pesto 35

Romesco Sauce 36

Chipotle Mayo 37

Baba Ghanoush 38

Spinach Artichoke Dip 39

CHAPTER 5: NUT BUTTERS AND SPREADS 40

Almond Butter 40

Cashew Butter 41

Chocolate Hazelnut Spread 42

Pumpkin Seed Butter 43

Pecan Butter 44

Coconut Almond Butter 45

Maple Cinnamon Almond Butter 46

Honey Roasted Peanut Butter 47

Sunflower Seed Butter 48

Walnut Butter 49

CHAPTER 6: FROZEN TREATS 50

Banana Ice Cream 50

Strawberry Sorbet 50

Tropical Fruit Popsicles 51

Chocolate Avocado Mousse 51

Mango Lassi Popsicles 52

Blueberry Coconut Ice Cream 52

Green Tea Matcha Ice Cream 53

Raspberry Lemonade Slushie 53

Peanut Butter Fudge Pops 54

Coconut Lime Granita 54

CHAPTER 7: JUICES AND TONICS 55

Green Juice 55

Beet and Ginger Tonic 55

Citrus Refresher 56

Carrot and Turmeric Elixir 56

Watermelon Mint Refresher 57

Apple Ginger Zinger 57

Pineapple Kale Kickstart 58

Berry Beet Blast 58

Cucumber Melon Cooler 59

Pomegranate Chia Fresca 59

CHAPTER 8: BABY AND TODDLER PUREES 60

Sweet Potato and Apple Baby Puree 60

Broccoli and Cheddar Toddler Puree 60

Banana and Blueberry Baby Puree 61

Spinach and Pear Baby Puree 61

Butternut Squash and Carrot Baby Puree 62

Peach and Oatmeal Baby Puree 62

Green Bean and Potato Toddler Puree 63

Mango and Yogurt Baby Puree 63

Avocado and Kiwi Baby Puree 64

Zucchini and Lentil Baby Puree 64

CHAPTER 9: BOOSTERS AND SUPERFOODS 65

Protein Powder Blends 65

Chia Seed Pudding 65

Acai Bowl 66

Turmeric Latte 66

Matcha Green Tea Smoothie 67

Spirulina Smoothie 67

Maca Root Energy Balls 68

Goji Berry Granola 68

Cacao Nibs Trail Mix 69

Flaxseed Crackers 69

CHAPTER 10: SAVORY SNACKS AND SIDES 70

Zucchini Fritters 70

Cauliflower Tots 71

Beet Hummus 72

Edamame Guacamole 73

Carrot and Parsnip Fries 74

Sweet Potato Falafels 75

Kale Chips 76

Black Bean Brownies 77

Broccoli Tots 78

Roasted Chickpeas 79

CONCLUSION 80

INTRODUCTION

Overview of the NutriBullet and its Benefits

When I was first trying to overhaul my eating habits and lose weight, I felt utterly lost and overwhelmed. Fad diets claimed to have all the answers, but their extreme restrictions left me feeling deprived and frustrated. After a few half-hearted attempts, I always found myself reverting to my old, unhealthy ways.

The turning point came when my best friend Jenny raved about the NutriBullet - a powerful little blender that was revolutionizing her morning routine. She couldn't stop talking about how energized she felt after having a nutrient-packed smoothie to start her day. As someone who usually skipped breakfast or grudgingly forced down a granola bar in the car, I was instantly intrigued.

I'll admit, I was a skeptic at first. How could throwing some fruits and veggies in a blender really make that much of a difference? But Jenny insisted I try her NutriBullet before passing judgment. One sip of her creamy mixed berry smoothie, and I was a convert. It was bursting with fresh, natural flavors unlike anything I'd ever tasted from a store-bought juice or milkshake.

Over the following weeks, I incorporated the NutriBullet into my daily routine and was amazed by the results. I had significantly more energy to power through my workdays. My skin glowed, and even my nails and hair looked healthier. Best of all, the pounds started melting away with ease. I no longer craved sugary, salty snacks or giant portions - the NutriBullet's nutritious blends kept me feeling fuller for longer.

So what exactly is this magic bullet blender, and why is it so effective? The key lies in its patented nutrient extraction technology and powerful 600-watt motor. Unlike typical blenders that simply blend ingredients together, the NutriBullet's specially designed blades extract every last drop of vitamins, minerals, enzymes and antioxidants from even the toughest ingredients like seeds, stems and skins. This "nutriblasting" process helps break down plant cells to maximize nutrition absorption.

The blender's tall pitcher design and cyclonic blending action also play a role. Ingredients are continually pulled toward the blades, ensuring a consistently smooth texture with each blend. No more chunks or separation! The NutriBullet effortlessly pulverizes even the most fibrous vegetables, frozen fruits and tough nuts or seeds into silky smooth shakes and smoothies.

Because the NutriBullet retains all the beneficial fiber from whole fruits and veggies, its nutrient-dense blends help you feel fuller for longer between meals. This makes it a powerful tool for weight loss and appetite control. The high fiber content also aids digestion and helps sweep away toxins for a gentle detox effect.

Unlike juicing, which removes most of the fiber, the NutriBullet allows you to easily consume more of the recommended 25-30 grams of fiber per day. This helps lower cholesterol, regulates blood sugar levels, and reduces your risk of certain cancers. An added bonus - fiber feeds the "good" probiotic bacteria in your gut, boosting immunity.

With the NutriBullet's straightforward assembly, one-step blending, and travel cup attachments, it's easy to prepare ultra-creamy smoothies, shakes, nut butters and dips in seconds before dashing out the door. No more skipping the most important meal of the day! The compact size also means the NutriBullet can find a home on even the most cramped kitchen counter.

From improving skin and hair health to aiding weight loss and reducing disease risk, the benefits of the NutriBullet are impressive to say the least. But at its core, this powerful blender helped me develop a new, healthier relationship with food that was impossible to achieve through restrictive dieting alone.

PURPOSE OF THE BOOK AND TARGET AUDIENCE

As someone who has experienced the life-changing effects of the NutriBullet firsthand, it is my passion to share this incredible tool and its delicious possibilities with as many people as possible. This book is a comprehensive guide that will empower you to easily incorporate nutrient-dense smoothies, shakes, dips, soups and more into your daily routine for whole-body health.

Whether you're hoping to shed excess weight, boost your energy levels, eliminate toxins, achieve glowing skin, or simply consume more antioxidant-rich fruits and vegetables, the NutriBullet can help you reach those goals in a sustainable, satisfying way. And with hundreds of decadent recipes that taste like milkshakes, it couldn't be easier to drink your way to better health.

This book is designed for NutriBullet novices and seasoned pros alike. For those who are new to the NutriBullet world, the introductory chapters will be your go-to resource, covering:

- The science and technology behind the NutriBullet's nutrient extraction abilities
- Step-by-step instructions for assembling, using and cleaning your NutriBullet
- Tips for selecting the right blades and cup combinations based on recipe type
- Essential safety guidelines to follow for optimal usage
- Tricks for modifying smoothie ingredients to suit dietary restrictions or taste preferences
- A handy guide to stocking your pantry with nutritious smoothie boosters
- Creative ideas for using the NutriBullet to whip up dips, nut butters, baby food and more

From there, we'll dive into 10 recipe chapters packed with easy, delicious and nutritionally balanced smoothies, shakes, nut milks, juices and other blends to enjoy for every meal and occasion. Wake up to a Chapter like "Breakfast Blasts" with dense, decadent options like Chunky Monkey Protein Smoothies, Chocolate Peanut Butter Banana Shakes, and Maple Pecan Oatmeal Smoothie Bowls.

During busy days, keep energized and satisfied with refreshing "Superfood Smoothies" like Blueberry Avocado Smoothies, Tropical Turmeric Tonics, Cacao Cherry Superchargers and Green Machine Smoothies. Kids and adults alike will be begging for seconds of the "Frozen Smoothie Pops & Bowls" with playful treats like Watermelon Slushies, Strawberry Cheesecake Protein Pops and Key Lime Pie Smoothies.

You'll also find hearty, savory blends to replace traditional meals in chapters like "Soups & Bisques" and "Velvety Vegan Blends" with recipes like Smoky Sweet Potato Soup, Gazpacho Shots, Cashew Cream of Broccoli Bisque and Portobello Fajita Burgers.

While the NutriBullet excels at whipping up wholesome, vitamin-packed beverages, it's also a fantastic tool for creating quick, homemade condiments and bases. Chapters like "Dips & Dressings," "Nut Butters & Seed Spreads" and "Sweet Treats & Snacks" will show you just how versatile this blender can be. Who knew you could easily make everything from Hummus, Salsa and Pesto to Cinnamon Almond Butter, Homemade Nutella and Edible Cookie Dough right in the NutriBullet?

For those with special dietary needs, you'll find an entire chapter dedicated to "Dietary Blends" with vegan, paleo, keto, and diabetic-friendly recipes to suit your lifestyle. There's also a dedicated section with "Kid-Approved Blends" for picky eaters of all ages, with hidden veggie smoothie masterpieces like Strawberry Smash Cake Shakes, "Jelly Donut" Smoothie Shots, and Creamy Orange Creamsicles.

Each recipe is nutritionally balanced and carefully calibrated for the ideal ratios of fruits, vegetables, proteins and healthy fats to keep you feeling full and energized for hours. But that doesn't mean these blends are austere or boring! Thanks to the NutriBullet's extract technology, naturally sweet fruits, rich nuts and decadent additions like cocoa powder, nut butters, spices and extracts achieve utterly craveable flavors.

Nearly all recipes include easy ingredient swaps and substitutions to accommodate allergies, food sensitivities or simply personal preferences. Many are inherently gluten-free, dairy-free and vegan. Detailed nutritional information is provided as well for those watching their calorie,

CHAPTER 1: BREAKFAST BLASTS

Green Smoothie Bowl

Prep: 10 mins | Serves: 2

Ingredients:

- US: 2 cups spinach leaves, 1 ripe banana, 1/2 avocado, 1/2 cup almond milk, 1 tablespoon chia seeds, 1/2 cup frozen pineapple chunks

- UK: 160g spinach leaves, 1 ripe banana, 1/2 avocado, 120ml almond milk, 15g chia seeds, 80g frozen pineapple chunks

Instructions:

1. Blend spinach, banana, avocado, almond milk, and chia seeds until smooth using your Nutribullet.

2. Pour the mixture into bowls.

3. Top with frozen pineapple chunks.

4. Enjoy your nutritious Green Smoothie Bowl!

Nutritional Info: Calories: 190 | Fat: 8g | Carbs: 30g | Protein: 5g

Tropical Fruit Parfait

Prep: 5 mins | Serves: 1

Ingredients:

- US: 1/2 cup Greek yogurt, 1/2 cup chopped mango, 1/2 cup chopped pineapple, 2 tablespoons shredded coconut

- UK: 120g Greek yogurt, 120g chopped mango, 120g chopped pineapple, 30g shredded coconut

Instructions:

1. Layer Greek yogurt, mango, and pineapple in a glass.

2. Sprinkle shredded coconut on top.

3. Repeat layering.

4. Serve immediately for a refreshing Tropical Fruit Parfait!

Nutritional Info: Calories: 320 | Fat: 12g | Carbs: 45g | Protein: 15g

Peanut Butter Banana Protein Shake

Prep: 5 mins | Serves: 1

Ingredients:

- US: 1 ripe banana, 1 tablespoon peanut butter, 1 scoop protein powder, 1 cup almond milk, ice cubes

- UK: 1 ripe banana, 15g peanut butter, 30g protein powder, 240ml almond milk, ice cubes

Instructions:

1. Combine banana, peanut butter, protein powder, almond milk, and ice cubes in your Nutribullet.

2. Blend until smooth.

3. Pour into a glass.

4. Enjoy your Peanut Butter Banana Protein Shake!

Nutritional Info: Calories: 350 | Fat: 10g | Carbs: 45g | Protein: 25g

Overnight Oats Smoothie

Prep: 5 mins | Serves: 1

Ingredients:

- US: 1/2 cup rolled oats, 1/2 cup Greek yogurt, 1/2 cup almond milk, 1 tablespoon honey, 1/2 teaspoon vanilla extract, 1/2 cup mixed berries

- UK: 40g rolled oats, 120g Greek yogurt, 120ml almond milk, 15g honey, 2.5ml vanilla extract, 80g mixed berries

Instructions:

1. Combine rolled oats, Greek yogurt, almond milk, honey, and vanilla extract in a jar.

2. Stir well, then cover and refrigerate overnight.

3. In the morning, blend the overnight oats with mixed berries until smooth.

4. Serve immediately or pour into a travel cup for a quick breakfast on the go!

Nutritional Info: Calories: 320 | Fat: 6g | Carbs: 55g | Protein: 15g

Berry Breakfast Blast

Prep: 5 mins | Serves: 2

Ingredients:

- US: 1 cup mixed berries (strawberries, blueberries, raspberries), 1 banana, 1/2 cup spinach leaves, 1 cup almond milk, 1 tablespoon honey

- UK: 160g mixed berries (strawberries, blueberries, raspberries), 1 banana, 40g spinach leaves, 240ml almond milk, 15g honey

Instructions:

1. Combine mixed berries, banana, spinach leaves, almond milk, and honey in your Nutribullet.

2. Blend until smooth.

3. Pour into glasses.

4. Enjoy your Berry Breakfast Blast!

Nutritional Info: Calories: 150 | Fat: 3g | Carbs: 30g | Protein: 3g

Tropical Green Machine

Prep: 5 mins | Serves: 1

Ingredients:

- US: 1/2 cup chopped pineapple, 1/2 cup chopped mango, 1 cup spinach leaves, 1/2 avocado, 1 tablespoon lime juice, 1/2 cup coconut water

- UK: 120g chopped pineapple, 120g chopped mango, 40g spinach leaves, 1/2 avocado, 15ml lime juice, 120ml coconut water

Instructions:

1. Blend pineapple, mango, spinach leaves, avocado, lime juice, and coconut water in your Nutribullet until smooth.

2. Pour into a glass.

3. Sip and enjoy your Tropical Green Machine!

Nutritional Info: Calories: 250 | Fat: 10g | Carbs: 40g | Protein: 5g

Cinnamon Roll Smoothie

Prep: 5 mins | Serves: 1

Ingredients:

- US: 1/2 cup Greek yogurt, 1/2 cup almond milk, 1/2 banana, 1/2 teaspoon ground cinnamon, 1 tablespoon honey, 1/4 teaspoon vanilla extract

- UK: 120g Greek yogurt, 120ml almond milk, 1/2 banana, 2.5ml ground cinnamon, 15g honey, 1.25ml vanilla extract

Instructions:

1. Blend Greek yogurt, almond milk, banana, ground cinnamon, honey, and vanilla extract until smooth.

2. Pour into a glass.

3. Sprinkle with a dash of cinnamon on top.

4. Indulge in the deliciousness of your Cinnamon Roll Smoothie!

Nutritional Info: Calories: 200 | Fat: 2g | Carbs: 40g | Protein: 15g

Carrot Cake Smoothie

Prep: 5 mins | Serves: 1

Ingredients:

- US: 1/2 cup shredded carrots, 1/2 banana, 1/4 cup rolled oats, 1/2 teaspoon ground cinnamon, 1/4 teaspoon ground nutmeg, 1 cup almond milk, 1 tablespoon maple syrup

- UK: 60g shredded carrots, 1/2 banana, 20g rolled oats, 2.5ml ground cinnamon, 1.25ml ground nutmeg, 240ml almond milk, 15ml maple syrup

Instructions:

1. Combine shredded carrots, banana, rolled oats, ground cinnamon, ground nutmeg, almond milk, and maple syrup in your Nutribullet.

2. Blend until smooth and creamy.

3. Pour into a glass.

4. Garnish with a sprinkle of cinnamon if desired.

5. Savor the flavors of a classic Carrot Cake Smoothie!

Nutritional Info: Calories: 220 | Fat: 3g | Carbs: 45g | Protein: 5g

Mocha Protein Smoothie

Prep: 5 mins | Serves: 1

Ingredients:

- US: 1/2 cup brewed coffee, cooled, 1/2 cup almond milk, 1 scoop chocolate protein powder, 1 tablespoon cocoa powder, 1 tablespoon maple syrup, ice cubes

- UK: 120ml brewed coffee, cooled, 120ml almond milk, 30g chocolate protein powder, 15g cocoa powder, 15ml maple syrup, ice cubes

Instructions:

1. Combine brewed coffee, almond milk, chocolate protein powder, cocoa powder, maple syrup, and ice cubes in your Nutribullet.

2. Blend until smooth and frothy.

3. Pour into a glass.

4. Sip and enjoy the rich flavors of your Mocha Protein Smoothie!

Nutritional Info: Calories: 200 | Fat: 5g | Carbs: 20g | Protein: 20g

Pumpkin Pie Smoothie

Prep: 5 mins | Serves: 1

Ingredients:

- US: 1/2 cup pumpkin puree, 1/2 banana, 1/2 cup Greek yogurt, 1/2 teaspoon pumpkin pie spice, 1 tablespoon honey, 1/2 cup almond milk, ice cubes

- UK: 120g pumpkin puree, 1/2 banana, 120g Greek yogurt, 2.5ml pumpkin pie spice, 15g honey, 120ml almond milk, ice cubes

Instructions:

1. Blend pumpkin puree, banana, Greek yogurt, pumpkin pie spice, honey, almond milk, and ice cubes in your Nutribullet until smooth.

2. Pour into a glass.

3. Sprinkle with a pinch of pumpkin pie spice on top for extra flavor.

4. Treat yourself to the taste of fall with your Pumpkin Pie Smoothie!

Nutritional Info: Calories: 220 | Fat: 3g | Carbs: 40g | Protein: 12g

CHAPTER 2: ENERGIZING SMOOTHIES

Berry Beet Refresher

Prep: 5 mins | Serves: 2

Ingredients:

- US: 1 cup mixed berries (strawberries, blueberries, raspberries), 1 small beet (peeled and chopped), 1 banana, 1 cup spinach leaves, 1 cup coconut water

- UK: 160g mixed berries (strawberries, blueberries, raspberries), 1 small beet (peeled and chopped), 1 banana, 40g spinach leaves, 240ml coconut water

Instructions:

1. Combine mixed berries, chopped beet, banana, spinach leaves, and coconut water in your Nutribullet.

2. Blend until smooth.

3. Pour into glasses.

4. Sip and feel refreshed with your Berry Beet Refresher!

Nutritional Info: Calories: 120 | Fat: 1g | Carbs: 30g | Protein: 3g

Mango Madness

Prep: 5 mins | Serves: 2

Ingredients:

- US: 2 ripe mangoes (peeled and chopped), 1 cup pineapple chunks, 1/2 cup Greek yogurt, 1 tablespoon honey, 1 cup almond milk

- UK: 2 ripe mangoes (peeled and chopped), 160g pineapple chunks, 120g Greek yogurt, 15g honey, 240ml almond milk

Instructions:

1. Blend ripe mangoes, pineapple chunks, Greek yogurt, honey, and almond milk in your Nutribullet until smooth.

2. Pour into glasses.

3. Indulge in the tropical flavors of Mango Madness!

Nutritional Info: Calories: 200 | Fat: 2g | Carbs: 45g | Protein: 5g

Green Machine

Prep: 5 mins | Serves: 1

Ingredients:

- US: 1 cup spinach leaves, 1/2 cucumber (peeled and chopped), 1/2 green apple (cored and chopped), 1/2 avocado, 1 tablespoon lemon juice, 1 cup coconut water

- UK: 40g spinach leaves, 1/2 cucumber (peeled and chopped), 1/2 green apple (cored and chopped), 1/2 avocado, 15ml lemon juice, 240ml coconut water

Instructions:

1. Blend spinach leaves, chopped cucumber, green apple, avocado, lemon juice, and coconut water in your Nutribullet until smooth.

2. Pour into a glass.

3. Enjoy the nutrient-packed goodness of Green Machine!

Nutritional Info: Calories: 180 | Fat: 5g | Carbs: 30g | Protein: 5g

Chocolate Peanut Butter Cup

Prep: 5 mins | Serves: 1

Ingredients:

- US: 1 banana, 1 tablespoon cocoa powder, 1 tablespoon peanut butter, 1/2 cup Greek yogurt, 1/2 cup almond milk, ice cubes

- UK: 1 banana, 15g cocoa powder, 15g peanut butter, 120g Greek yogurt, 120ml almond milk, ice cubes

Instructions:

1. Combine banana, cocoa powder, peanut butter, Greek yogurt, almond milk, and ice cubes in your Nutribullet.

2. Blend until creamy and smooth.

3. Pour into a glass.

4. Savour the indulgent taste of Chocolate Peanut Butter Cup!

Nutritional Info: Calories: 250 | Fat: 8g | Carbs: 40g | Protein: 15g

Citrus Zinger

Prep: 5 mins | Serves: 2

Ingredients:

- US: 2 oranges (peeled and segmented), 1 grapefruit (peeled and segmented), 1 lime (juiced), 1 tablespoon honey, 1 cup coconut water

- UK: 2 oranges (peeled and segmented), 1 grapefruit (peeled and segmented), 1 lime (juiced), 15g honey, 240ml coconut water

Instructions:

1. Blend orange segments, grapefruit segments, lime juice, honey, and coconut water in your Nutribullet until smooth.

2. Pour into glasses.

3. Enjoy the tangy freshness of Citrus Zinger!

Nutritional Info: Calories: 150 | Fat: 1g | Carbs: 35g | Protein: 2g

Blueberry Almond Delight

Prep: 5 mins | Serves: 1

Ingredients:

- US: 1/2 cup blueberries, 1/4 cup almonds, 1 banana, 1/2 cup Greek yogurt, 1/2 cup almond milk, ice cubes

- UK: 80g blueberries, 30g almonds, 1 banana, 120g Greek yogurt, 120ml almond milk, ice cubes

Instructions:

1. Blend blueberries, almonds, banana, Greek yogurt, almond milk, and ice cubes in your Nutribullet until smooth.

2. Pour into a glass.

3. Sip and enjoy the delightful blend of Blueberry Almond Delight!

Nutritional Info: Calories: 280 | Fat: 10g | Carbs: 35g | Protein: 15g

Kale Pineapple Energizer

Prep: 5 mins | Serves: 1

Ingredients:

- US: 1 cup kale leaves, 1/2 cup pineapple chunks, 1/2 banana, 1/2 cup coconut water, 1 tablespoon lime juice, ice cubes

- UK: 40g kale leaves, 80g pineapple chunks, 1/2 banana, 120ml coconut water, 15ml lime juice, ice cubes

Instructions:

1. Blend kale leaves, pineapple chunks, banana, coconut water, lime juice, and ice cubes in your Nutribullet until smooth.

2. Pour into a glass.

3. Feel the energizing power of Kale Pineapple Energizer!

Nutritional Info: Calories: 150 | Fat: 1g | Carbs: 35g | Protein: 3g

Strawberry Banana Blast

Prep: 5 mins | Serves: 2

Ingredients:

- US: 1 cup strawberries, 1 banana, 1/2 cup Greek yogurt, 1/2 cup almond milk, 1 tablespoon honey, ice cubes

- UK: 160g strawberries, 1 banana, 120g Greek yogurt, 120ml almond milk, 15g honey, ice cubes

Instructions:

1. Blend strawberries, banana, Greek yogurt, almond milk, honey, and ice cubes in your Nutribullet until smooth.

2. Pour into glasses.

3. Enjoy the fruity goodness of Strawberry Banana Blast!

Nutritional Info: Calories: 200 | Fat: 2g | Carbs: 45g | Protein: 5g

Coconut Cashew Crave

Prep: 5 mins | Serves: 1

Ingredients:

- US: 1/2 cup coconut milk, 1/4 cup cashews, 1/2 banana, 1 tablespoon shredded coconut, 1 tablespoon maple syrup, ice cubes

- UK: 120ml coconut milk, 30g cashews, 1/2 banana, 15g shredded coconut, 15ml maple syrup, ice cubes

Instructions:

1. Blend coconut milk, cashews, banana, shredded coconut, maple syrup, and ice cubes in your Nutribullet until creamy.

2. Pour into a glass.

3. Savour the tropical delight of Coconut Cashew Crave!

Nutritional Info: Calories: 320 | Fat: 20g | Carbs: 30g | Protein: 5g

Ginger Peach Punch

Prep: 5 mins | Serves: 2

Ingredients:

- US: 2 ripe peaches (pitted and chopped), 1/2 inch fresh ginger (peeled and chopped), 1/2 cup Greek yogurt, 1 tablespoon honey, 1 cup almond milk, ice cubes

- UK: 2 ripe peaches (pitted and chopped), 1.25cm fresh ginger (peeled and chopped), 120g Greek yogurt, 15g honey, 240ml almond milk, ice cubes

Instructions:

1. Blend ripe peaches, fresh ginger, Greek yogurt, honey, almond milk, and ice cubes in your Nutribullet until smooth.

2. Pour into glasses.

3. Enjoy the refreshing kick of Ginger Peach Punch!

Nutritional Info: Calories: 200 | Fat: 2g | Carbs: 40g | Protein: 5g

CHAPTER 3: SOUPS AND STEWS

Creamy Tomato Soup

Prep: 10 mins | Cook: 20 mins | Serves: 4

Ingredients:

- US: 800g ripe tomatoes, 1 onion, 2 cloves garlic, 2 tablespoons olive oil, 1 tablespoon tomato paste, 500ml vegetable broth, 1/2 cup heavy cream, salt, pepper, fresh basil leaves (for garnish)

- UK: 800g ripe tomatoes, 1 onion, 2 cloves garlic, 30ml olive oil, 15g tomato paste, 500ml vegetable broth, 120ml heavy cream, salt, pepper, fresh basil leaves (for garnish)

Instructions:

1. Heat olive oil in a large saucepan over medium heat.

2. Add chopped onion and minced garlic. Sauté until softened.

3. Stir in tomato paste and cook for another minute.

4. Add chopped tomatoes and vegetable broth. Bring to a simmer and cook for 15 minutes.

5. Blend the soup until smooth using your Nutribullet.

6. Return the soup to the saucepan over low heat.

7. Stir in heavy cream and season with salt and pepper to taste.

8. Simmer for another 5 minutes, then serve hot, garnished with fresh basil leaves.

Nutritional Info: Calories: 220 | Fat: 18g | Carbs: 15g | Protein: 4g

Butternut Squash Bisque

Prep: 15 mins | Cook: 30 mins | Serves: 4

Ingredients:

- US: 1 medium butternut squash, 1 onion, 2 cloves garlic, 1 tablespoon olive oil, 1 teaspoon ground cinnamon, 1/2 teaspoon ground nutmeg, 500ml vegetable broth, 1/2 cup coconut milk, salt, pepper, fresh thyme (for garnish)

- UK: 1 medium butternut squash, 1 onion, 2 cloves garlic, 15ml olive oil, 5ml ground cinnamon, 2.5ml ground nutmeg, 500ml vegetable broth, 120ml coconut milk, salt, pepper, fresh thyme (for garnish)

Instructions:

1. Preheat your oven to 200°C (400°F).

2. Peel and cube the butternut squash. Chop the onion and mince the garlic.

3. Place the squash, onion, and garlic on a baking sheet. Drizzle with olive oil and sprinkle with cinnamon, nutmeg, salt, and pepper. Toss to coat evenly.

4. Roast in the preheated oven for 25-30 minutes until tender and caramelized.

5. Transfer the roasted vegetables to a saucepan. Add vegetable broth and coconut milk. Bring to a simmer.

6. Blend the mixture until smooth using your Nutribullet.

7. Return the bisque to the saucepan. Season with salt and pepper to taste.

8. Simmer for another 5 minutes, then serve hot, garnished with fresh thyme.

Nutritional Info: Calories: 180 | Fat: 8g | Carbs: 25g | Protein: 3g

Chilled Gazpacho

Prep: 15 mins | Chill: 1 hour | Serves: 4

Ingredients:

- US: 4 large ripe tomatoes, 1 cucumber, 1 red bell pepper, 1 small red onion, 2 cloves garlic, 2 tablespoons olive oil, 2 tablespoons red wine vinegar, 1 teaspoon Worcestershire sauce, salt, pepper, fresh parsley (for garnish)

- UK: 4 large ripe tomatoes, 1 cucumber, 1 red bell pepper, 1 small red onion, 2 cloves garlic, 30ml olive oil, 30ml red wine vinegar, 5ml Worcestershire sauce, salt, pepper, fresh parsley (for garnish)

Instructions:

1. Chop tomatoes, cucumber, bell pepper, and red onion into chunks.

2. Mince garlic cloves.

3. Combine all chopped vegetables in a large bowl.

4. Add olive oil, red wine vinegar, and Worcestershire sauce. Season with salt and pepper to taste.

5. Blend the mixture until smooth using your Nutribullet.

6. Transfer the gazpacho to a large container and chill in the refrigerator for at least 1 hour.

7. Serve the chilled gazpacho in bowls, garnished with fresh parsley.

Nutritional Info: Calories: 120 | Fat: 7g | Carbs: 15g | Protein: 3g

Hearty Lentil Stew

Prep: 10 mins | Cook: 40 mins | Serves: 6

Ingredients:

- US: 1 cup dried green lentils, 1 onion, 2 carrots, 2 stalks celery, 2 cloves garlic, 1 can diced tomatoes, 1 tablespoon tomato paste, 1 teaspoon ground cumin, 1 teaspoon smoked paprika, 1/2 teaspoon dried thyme, 4 cups vegetable broth, salt, pepper, fresh parsley (for garnish)

- UK: 200g dried green lentils, 1 onion, 2 carrots, 2 stalks celery, 2 cloves garlic, 400g can diced tomatoes, 15g tomato paste, 5ml ground cumin, 5ml smoked paprika, 2.5ml dried thyme, 1 litre vegetable broth, salt, pepper, fresh parsley (for garnish)

Instructions:

1. Rinse the lentils under cold water and set aside.

2. Chop onion, carrots, celery, and mince garlic.

3. Heat olive oil in a large pot over medium heat.

4. Sauté onion, carrots, celery, and garlic until softened.

5. Stir in tomato paste, cumin, paprika, and thyme. Cook for 1-2 minutes.

6. Add diced tomatoes, lentils, and vegetable broth to the pot. Bring to a boil, then reduce heat and simmer for 30-35 minutes until lentils are tender.

7. Season with salt and pepper to taste.

8. Serve hot, garnished with fresh parsley.

Nutritional Info: Calories: 250 | Fat: 2g | Carbs: 45g | Protein: 15g

Broccoli Cheddar Soup

Prep: 10 mins | Cook: 20 mins | Serves: 4

Ingredients:

- US: 2 cups broccoli florets, 1 onion, 2 cloves garlic, 2 tablespoons butter, 2 tablespoons all-purpose flour, 2 cups vegetable broth, 1 cup milk, 1 cup shredded cheddar cheese, salt, pepper, nutmeg, fresh chives (for garnish)

- UK: 160g broccoli florets, 1 onion, 2 cloves garlic, 30g butter, 30g all-purpose flour, 480ml vegetable broth, 240ml milk, 120g shredded cheddar cheese, salt, pepper, nutmeg, fresh chives (for garnish)

Instructions:

1. Chop the onion and mince the garlic.
2. Steam the broccoli until tender.
3. In a large pot, melt the butter over medium heat.
4. Add the chopped onion and minced garlic. Sauté until softened.
5. Sprinkle the flour over the onions and garlic. Stir constantly for 1-2 minutes.
6. Gradually pour in the vegetable broth while stirring continuously to avoid lumps.
7. Add the milk and continue stirring until the mixture thickens.
8. Stir in the steamed broccoli and shredded cheddar cheese until the cheese melts and the soup is smooth.
9. Season with salt, pepper, and a pinch of nutmeg to taste.
10. Serve hot, garnished with fresh chives.

Nutritional Info: Calories: 280 | Fat: 18g | Carbs: 20g | Protein: 12g

Carrot Ginger Soup

Prep: 10 mins | Cook: 25 mins | Serves: 4

Ingredients:

- US: 500g carrots, 1 onion, 2 cloves garlic, 1 tablespoon olive oil, 1 tablespoon grated ginger, 4 cups vegetable broth, 1/2 cup coconut milk, salt, pepper, fresh cilantro (for garnish)

- UK: 500g carrots, 1 onion, 2 cloves garlic, 15ml olive oil, 15ml grated ginger, 1 litre vegetable broth, 120ml coconut milk, salt, pepper, fresh cilantro (for garnish)

Instructions:

1. Peel and chop the carrots, chop the onion, and mince the garlic.

2. Heat olive oil in a large pot over medium heat.

3. Add the chopped onion and minced garlic. Sauté until softened.

4. Stir in grated ginger and cook for another minute.

5. Add chopped carrots and vegetable broth to the pot. Bring to a boil, then reduce heat and simmer for 20 minutes until carrots are tender.

6. Blend the soup until smooth using your Nutribullet.

7. Return the soup to the pot. Stir in coconut milk and season with salt and pepper to taste.

8. Simmer for another 5 minutes.

9. Serve hot, garnished with fresh cilantro.

Nutritional Info: Calories: 180 | Fat: 10g | Carbs: 20g | Protein: 3g

Black Bean Soup

Prep: 10 mins | Cook: 25 mins | Serves: 4

Ingredients:

- US: 2 cans black beans, 1 onion, 2 cloves garlic, 1 red bell pepper, 1 teaspoon ground cumin, 1 teaspoon chili powder, 4 cups vegetable broth, 1/4 cup fresh lime juice, salt, pepper, fresh cilantro (for garnish)

- UK: 2 cans black beans, 1 onion, 2 cloves garlic, 1 red bell pepper, 5ml ground cumin, 5ml chili powder, 1 litre vegetable broth, 60ml fresh lime juice, salt, pepper, fresh cilantro (for garnish)

Instructions:

1. Chop the onion, mince the garlic, and dice the red bell pepper.

2. In a large pot, combine one can of black beans (undrained), chopped onion, minced garlic, diced red bell pepper, ground cumin, chili powder, and vegetable broth.

3. Bring to a boil, then reduce heat and simmer for 15 minutes.

4. Blend the soup until smooth using your Nutribullet.

5. Return the soup to the pot. Stir in the second can of black beans (drained and rinsed) and fresh lime juice.

6. Season with salt and pepper to taste.

7. Simmer for another 10 minutes.

8. Serve hot, garnished with fresh cilantro.

Nutritional Info: Calories: 220 | Fat: 1g | Carbs: 40g | Protein: 12g

Roasted Red Pepper Soup

Prep: 10 mins | Cook: 30 mins | Serves: 4

Ingredients:

- US: 4 red bell peppers, 1 onion, 2 cloves garlic, 2 tablespoons olive oil, 4 cups vegetable broth, 1/2 cup heavy cream, salt, pepper, smoked paprika, fresh basil leaves (for garnish)

- UK: 4 red bell peppers, 1 onion, 2 cloves garlic, 30ml olive oil, 1 litre vegetable broth, 120ml heavy cream, salt, pepper, smoked paprika, fresh basil leaves (for garnish)

Instructions:

1. Preheat your oven to 200°C (400°F).

2. Halve and seed the red bell peppers. Place them cut-side down on a baking sheet.

3. Roast the peppers in the preheated oven for 20-25 minutes until the skins are charred.

4. Remove the peppers from the oven and transfer them to a bowl. Cover with plastic wrap and let steam for 10 minutes.

5. Peel off the skins from the peppers and chop them into chunks.

6. Chop the onion and mince the garlic.

7. Heat olive oil in a large pot over medium heat.

8. Add chopped onion and minced garlic. Sauté until softened.

9. Stir in chopped roasted red peppers and vegetable broth. Bring to a boil, then reduce heat and simmer for 15 minutes.

10. Blend the soup until smooth using your Nutribullet.

11. Return the soup to the pot. Stir in heavy cream and season with salt, pepper, and a pinch of smoked paprika to taste.

12. Simmer for another 5 minutes.

13. Serve hot, garnished with fresh basil leaves.

Nutritional Info: Calories: 220 | Fat: 16g | Carbs: 18g | Protein: 4g

Sweet Potato Coconut Curry Soup

Prep: 15 mins | Cook: 25 mins | Serves: 4

Ingredients:

- US: 2 large sweet potatoes, 1 onion, 2 cloves garlic, 1 tablespoon curry powder, 1 can coconut milk, 4 cups vegetable broth, 2 tablespoons olive oil, salt, pepper, fresh cilantro (for garnish)

- UK: 2 large sweet potatoes, 1 onion, 2 cloves garlic, 15ml curry powder, 1 can coconut milk, 1 litre vegetable broth, 30ml olive oil, salt, pepper, fresh cilantro (for garnish)

Instructions:

1. Peel and cube the sweet potatoes, chop the onion, and mince the garlic.

2. Heat olive oil in a large pot over medium heat.

3. Add chopped onion and minced garlic. Sauté until softened.

4. Stir in curry powder and cook for another minute.

5. Add cubed sweet potatoes, coconut milk, and vegetable broth to the pot. Bring to a boil, then reduce heat and simmer for 20 minutes until sweet potatoes are tender.

6. Blend the soup until smooth using your Nutribullet.

7. Return the soup to the pot. Season with salt and pepper to taste.

8. Simmer for another 5 minutes.

9. Serve hot, garnished with fresh cilantro.

Nutritional Info: Calories: 280 | Fat: 20g | Carbs: 25g | Protein: 4g

Minestrone Soup

Prep: 15 mins | Cook: 30 mins | Serves: 6

Ingredients:

- US: 2 carrots, 2 celery stalks, 1 onion, 2 cloves garlic, 1 zucchini, 1 can diced tomatoes, 1 can kidney beans, 1/2 cup small pasta, 4 cups vegetable broth, 2 tablespoons olive oil, salt, pepper, fresh parsley (for garnish)

- UK: 2 carrots, 2 celery stalks, 1 onion, 2 cloves garlic, 1 zucchini, 400g can diced tomatoes, 400g can kidney beans, 120g small pasta, 1 litre vegetable broth, 30ml olive oil, salt, pepper, fresh parsley (for garnish)

Instructions:

1. Chop carrots, celery, onion, garlic, and zucchini into small pieces.

2. Heat olive oil in a large pot over medium heat.

3. Add chopped onion and minced garlic. Sauté until softened.

4. Stir in chopped carrots, celery, and zucchini. Cook for 5 minutes.

5. Add diced tomatoes, kidney beans, small pasta, and vegetable broth to the pot.

6. Bring to a boil, then reduce heat and simmer for 20 minutes until vegetables are tender and pasta is cooked.

7. Season with salt and pepper to taste.

8. Serve hot, garnished with fresh parsley.

Nutritional Info: Calories: 240 | Fat: 6g | Carbs: 38g | Protein: 9g

CHAPTER 4: SAUCES AND DIPS

Guacamole

Prep: 10 mins | Serves: 4

Ingredients:

- US: 2 ripe avocados, 1 tomato, 1/4 onion, 1 lime, 1/4 cup cilantro, salt, pepper

- UK: 2 ripe avocados, 1 tomato, 1/4 onion, 1 lime, 15g cilantro, salt, pepper

Instructions:

1. Halve and pit the avocados, then scoop the flesh into a bowl.

2. Dice the tomato and finely chop the onion and cilantro.

3. Add the diced tomato, chopped onion, and cilantro to the bowl with the avocado.

4. Squeeze the lime juice over the mixture.

5. Season with salt and pepper to taste.

6. Mash everything together until desired consistency using your Nutribullet.

7. Serve with tortilla chips or use as a topping for tacos and salads.

Nutritional Info: Calories: 120 | Fat: 10g | Carbs: 7g | Protein: 2g

Hummus

Prep: 10 mins | Serves: 6

Ingredients:

- US: 1 can (400g) chickpeas, 2 cloves garlic, 1/4 cup tahini, 2 tablespoons lemon juice, 2 tablespoons olive oil, salt, pepper

- UK: 1 can (400g) chickpeas, 2 cloves garlic, 60g tahini, 30ml lemon juice, 30ml olive oil, salt, pepper

Instructions:

1. Rinse and drain the chickpeas.

2. Peel the garlic cloves.

3. Combine chickpeas, garlic, tahini, lemon juice, and olive oil in your Nutribullet.

4. Season with salt and pepper to taste.

5. Blend until smooth and creamy, adding a little water if needed to reach desired consistency.

6. Transfer to a serving bowl and drizzle with olive oil before serving.

Nutritional Info: Calories: 160 | Fat: 10g | Carbs: 14g | Protein: 5g

Salsa

Prep: 10 mins | Serves: 4

Ingredients:

- US: 4 ripe tomatoes, 1/4 onion, 1 jalapeño pepper, 1/4 cup cilantro, 1 lime, salt, pepper

- UK: 4 ripe tomatoes, 1/4 onion, 1 jalapeño pepper, 15g cilantro, 1 lime, salt, pepper

Instructions:

1. Dice the tomatoes and finely chop the onion, jalapeño pepper, and cilantro.

2. Combine diced tomatoes, chopped onion, chopped jalapeño, and chopped cilantro in a bowl.

3. Squeeze the lime juice over the mixture.

4. Season with salt and pepper to taste.

5. Stir everything together until well combined.

6. Serve with tortilla chips or as a topping for tacos and grilled meats.

Nutritional Info: Calories: 30 | Fat: 0g | Carbs: 7g | Protein: 1g

Cashew Cheese Sauce

Prep: 5 mins | Cook: 10 mins | Serves: 4

Ingredients:

- US: 1 cup cashews, 1/2 cup nutritional yeast, 1 teaspoon garlic powder, 1 teaspoon onion powder, 1 tablespoon lemon juice, 1 cup water, salt, pepper

- UK: 120g cashews, 60g nutritional yeast, 5ml garlic powder, 5ml onion powder, 15ml lemon juice, 240ml water, salt, pepper

Instructions:

1. Soak cashews in hot water for 30 minutes, then drain.

2. Combine soaked cashews, nutritional yeast, garlic powder, onion powder, lemon juice, and water in your Nutribullet.

3. Season with salt and pepper to taste.

4. Blend until smooth and creamy, adding more water if needed to reach desired consistency.

5. Transfer to a saucepan and heat over medium-low heat until warmed through.

6. Serve as a dip for veggies or drizzle over nachos and baked potatoes.

Nutritional Info: Calories: 150 | Fat: 10g | Carbs: 8g | Protein: 7g

Tzatziki Sauce

Prep: 10 mins | Serves: 4

Ingredients:

- US: 1 cucumber, 1 cup Greek yogurt, 2 cloves garlic, 1 tablespoon lemon juice, 1 tablespoon fresh dill, salt, pepper, olive oil

- UK: 1 cucumber, 240g Greek yogurt, 2 cloves garlic, 15ml lemon juice, 15ml fresh dill, salt, pepper, olive oil

Instructions:

1. Grate the cucumber and squeeze out excess moisture using a clean kitchen towel.

2. Mince the garlic cloves and chop the fresh dill.

3. In a bowl, combine grated cucumber, Greek yogurt, minced garlic, chopped dill, and lemon juice.

4. Season with salt and pepper to taste.

5. Drizzle with a little olive oil and stir until well combined.

6. Refrigerate for at least 30 minutes to allow flavors to meld.

7. Serve chilled as a dip with pita bread, veggies, or as a sauce for grilled meats.

Nutritional Info: Calories: 60 | Fat: 3g | Carbs: 4g | Protein: 5g

Pesto

Prep: 10 mins | Serves: 4

Ingredients:

- US: 2 cups fresh basil leaves, 1/2 cup pine nuts, 1/2 cup grated Parmesan cheese, 2 cloves garlic, 1/4 cup olive oil, salt, pepper

- UK: 50g fresh basil leaves, 60g pine nuts, 60g grated Parmesan cheese, 2 cloves garlic, 60ml olive oil, salt, pepper

Instructions:

1. Toast the pine nuts in a dry skillet over medium heat until lightly golden, then cool.

2. In a food processor or Nutribullet, combine fresh basil leaves, toasted pine nuts, grated Parmesan cheese, and minced garlic cloves.

3. Pulse until finely chopped.

4. While pulsing, slowly pour in olive oil until the pesto reaches desired consistency.

5. Season with salt and pepper to taste.

6. Transfer to a jar or container and store in the refrigerator.

7. Serve tossed with pasta, spread on sandwiches, or as a dip for bread.

Nutritional Info: Calories: 180 | Fat: 18g | Carbs: 2g | Protein: 4g

Romesco Sauce

Prep: 15 mins | Cook: 15 mins | Serves: 6

Ingredients:

- US: 2 roasted red bell peppers, 1/2 cup almonds, 2 cloves garlic, 2 tablespoons tomato paste, 2 tablespoons red wine vinegar, 1/4 cup olive oil, salt, pepper

- UK: 2 roasted red bell peppers, 60g almonds, 2 cloves garlic, 30ml tomato paste, 30ml red wine vinegar, 60ml olive oil, salt, pepper

Instructions:

1. Roast the red bell peppers until charred, then peel and seed them.

2. In a blender or Nutribullet, combine roasted red bell peppers, almonds, minced garlic, tomato paste, and red wine vinegar.

3. Blend until smooth, gradually adding olive oil until desired consistency is reached.

4. Season with salt and pepper to taste.

5. Transfer to a saucepan and heat over low heat until warmed through.

6. Serve as a dip, sauce for grilled meats, or spread on sandwiches.

Nutritional Info: Calories: 160 | Fat: 15g | Carbs: 5g | Protein: 4g

Chipotle Mayo

Prep: 5 mins | Serves: 4

Ingredients:

- US: 1/2 cup mayonnaise, 1 tablespoon adobo sauce (from canned chipotle peppers), 1 teaspoon lime juice, salt, pepper

- UK: 120ml mayonnaise, 15ml adobo sauce (from canned chipotle peppers), 5ml lime juice, salt, pepper

Instructions:

1. In a bowl, whisk together mayonnaise, adobo sauce, and lime juice until smooth.

2. Season with salt and pepper to taste.

3. Adjust the amount of adobo sauce according to desired spiciness.

4. Serve as a dipping sauce for fries, onion rings, or as a spread for sandwiches and burgers.

Nutritional Info: Calories: 100 | Fat: 10g | Carbs: 1g | Protein: 0g

Baba Ghanoush

Prep: 15 mins | Cook: 20 mins | Serves: 4

Ingredients:

- US: 2 medium eggplants, 2 cloves garlic, 2 tablespoons tahini, 2 tablespoons lemon juice, 2 tablespoons olive oil, salt, pepper

- UK: 2 medium eggplants, 2 cloves garlic, 30ml tahini, 30ml lemon juice, 30ml olive oil, salt, pepper

Instructions:

1. Preheat the oven to 200°C (400°F). Pierce the eggplants several times with a fork.

2. Roast the eggplants on a baking sheet for 20-25 minutes until soft and collapsed.

3. Cool slightly, then peel off the skins and discard.

4. In a food processor or Nutribullet, combine roasted eggplant flesh, minced garlic, tahini, and lemon juice.

5. Blend until smooth.

6. While blending, slowly drizzle in olive oil until creamy.

7. Season with salt and pepper to taste.

8. Transfer to a serving bowl and refrigerate for at least 1 hour before serving.

Nutritional Info: Calories: 120 | Fat: 10g | Carbs: 8g | Protein: 2g

Spinach Artichoke Dip

Prep: 10 mins | Cook: 25 mins | Serves: 6

Ingredients:

- US: 1 cup frozen chopped spinach, 1 can (400g) artichoke hearts, 1 cup cream cheese, 1/2 cup sour cream, 1/2 cup mayonnaise, 1 cup grated Parmesan cheese, 2 cloves garlic, salt, pepper

- UK: 150g frozen chopped spinach, 1 can (400g) artichoke hearts, 240g cream cheese, 120ml sour cream, 120ml mayonnaise, 120g grated Parmesan cheese **Instructions:**

1. Preheat your oven to 180°C (350°F).

2. Thaw and drain the chopped spinach, and drain the canned artichoke hearts. Chop the artichoke hearts into smaller pieces.

3. In a mixing bowl, combine the chopped spinach, chopped artichoke hearts, cream cheese, sour cream, mayonnaise, grated Parmesan cheese, and minced garlic cloves.

4. Season with salt and pepper to taste.

5. Mix until well combined.

6. Transfer the mixture to a baking dish and spread it out evenly.

7. Bake in the preheated oven for 20-25 minutes, or until the dip is bubbly and golden on top.

8. Remove from the oven and let it cool for a few minutes before serving.

9. Serve the spinach artichoke dip warm with tortilla chips, bread slices, or vegetable sticks.

Nutritional Info: Calories: 280 | Fat: 22g | Carbs: 7g | Protein: 12g

CHAPTER 5: NUT BUTTERS AND SPREADS

Almond Butter

Prep: 10 mins | Cook: 10 mins | Serves: 8

Ingredients:

- US: 500g almonds, salt (optional)

- UK: 500g almonds, salt (optional)

Instructions:

1. Preheat your oven to 175°C (350°F).

2. Spread almonds evenly on a baking sheet.

3. Roast almonds for 8-10 minutes until fragrant and lightly golden.

4. Allow the almonds to cool slightly.

5. Transfer the roasted almonds to your Nutribullet.

6. Blend until smooth and creamy, scraping down the sides as needed.

7. Add salt to taste if desired.

8. Transfer the almond butter to a jar or container.

9. Store in the refrigerator for up to 2 weeks.

Nutritional Info: Calories: 180 | Fat: 15g | Carbs: 7g | Protein: 7g

Cashew Butter

Prep: 10 mins | Cook: 10 mins | Serves: 8

Ingredients:

- US: 500g cashews, salt (optional)

- UK: 500g cashews, salt (optional)

Instructions:

1. Preheat your oven to 175°C (350°F).

2. Spread cashews evenly on a baking sheet.

3. Roast cashews for 8-10 minutes until lightly golden and fragrant.

4. Allow the cashews to cool slightly.

5. Transfer the roasted cashews to your Nutribullet.

6. Blend until smooth and creamy, scraping down the sides as needed.

7. Add salt to taste if desired.

8. Transfer the cashew butter to a jar or container.

9. Store in the refrigerator for up to 2 weeks.

Nutritional Info: Calories: 180 | Fat: 15g | Carbs: 8g | Protein: 6g

Chocolate Hazelnut Spread

Prep: 15 mins | Cook: 10 mins | Serves: 8

Ingredients:

- US: 250g hazelnuts, 2 tablespoons cocoa powder, 3 tablespoons powdered sugar, 2 tablespoons coconut oil, salt

- UK: 250g hazelnuts, 30g cocoa powder, 45g powdered sugar, 30g coconut oil, salt

Instructions:

1. Preheat your oven to 175°C (350°F).

2. Spread hazelnuts evenly on a baking sheet.

3. Roast hazelnuts for 8-10 minutes until fragrant and skins start to loosen.

4. Allow the hazelnuts to cool slightly, then rub them in a clean kitchen towel to remove the skins.

5. Transfer the peeled hazelnuts to your Nutribullet.

6. Add cocoa powder, powdered sugar, coconut oil, and a pinch of salt.

7. Blend until smooth and creamy, scraping down the sides as needed.

8. Transfer the chocolate hazelnut spread to a jar or container.

9. Store at room temperature for up to 2 weeks.

Nutritional Info: Calories: 200 | Fat: 17g | Carbs: 10g | Protein: 4g

Pumpkin Seed Butter

Prep: 10 mins | Cook: 10 mins | Serves: 8

Ingredients:

- US: 500g pumpkin seeds (pepitas), salt (optional)

- UK: 500g pumpkin seeds (pepitas), salt (optional)

Instructions:

1. Toast the pumpkin seeds in a dry skillet over medium heat for 5-7 minutes, stirring frequently, until fragrant and lightly golden.

2. Allow the toasted pumpkin seeds to cool slightly.

3. Transfer the pumpkin seeds to your Nutribullet.

4. Blend until smooth and creamy, scraping down the sides as needed.

5. Add salt to taste if desired.

6. Transfer the pumpkin seed butter to a jar or container.

7. Store in the refrigerator for up to 2 weeks.

Nutritional Info: Calories: 180 | Fat: 15g | Carbs: 4g | Protein: 9g

Pecan Butter

Prep: 10 mins | Cook: 10 mins | Serves: 8

Ingredients:

- US: 500g pecans, salt (optional)

- UK: 500g pecans, salt (optional)

Instructions:

1. Toast the pecans in a dry skillet over medium heat for 5-7 minutes, stirring frequently, until fragrant and lightly toasted.

2. Allow the toasted pecans to cool slightly.

3. Transfer the pecans to your Nutribullet.

4. Blend until smooth and creamy, scraping down the sides as needed.

5. Add salt to taste if desired.

6. Transfer the pecan butter to a jar or container.

7. Store in the refrigerator for up to 2 weeks.

Nutritional Info: Calories: 200 | Fat: 20g | Carbs: 4g | Protein: 4g

Coconut Almond Butter

Prep: 10 mins | Cook: 10 mins | Serves: 8

Ingredients:

- US: 250g almonds, 250g unsweetened shredded coconut, salt (optional)

- UK: 250g almonds, 250g unsweetened shredded coconut, salt (optional)

Instructions:

1. Toast the almonds and shredded coconut in a dry skillet over medium heat for 5-7 minutes, stirring frequently, until lightly golden.

2. Allow the toasted almonds and coconut to cool slightly.

3. Transfer the almonds and coconut to your Nutribullet.

4. Blend until smooth and creamy, scraping down the sides as needed.

5. Add salt to taste if desired.

6. Transfer the coconut almond butter to a jar or container.

7. Store in the refrigerator for up to 2 weeks.

Nutritional Info: Calories: 200 | Fat: 18g | Carbs: 8g | Protein: 6g

Maple Cinnamon Almond Butter

Prep: 10 mins | Cook: 10 mins | Serves: 8

Ingredients:

- US: 500g almonds, 2 tablespoons maple syrup, 1 teaspoon ground cinnamon, salt (optional)

- UK: 500g almonds, 30ml maple syrup, 5ml ground cinnamon, salt (optional)

Instructions:

1. Toast the almonds in a dry skillet over medium heat for 5-7 minutes, stirring frequently, until fragrant and lightly golden.

2. Allow the toasted almonds to cool slightly.

3. Transfer the almonds to your Nutribullet.

4. Add maple syrup, ground cinnamon, and a pinch of salt.

5. Blend until smooth and creamy, scraping down the sides as needed.

6. Transfer the maple cinnamon almond butter to a jar or container.

7. Store in the refrigerator for up to 2 weeks.

Nutritional Info: Calories: 200 | Fat: 18g | Carbs: 8g | Protein: 6g

Honey Roasted Peanut Butter

Prep: 10 mins | Cook: 15 mins | Serves: 8

Ingredients:

- US: 500g peanuts (unsalted), 2 tablespoons honey, salt (optional)

- UK: 500g peanuts (unsalted), 30ml honey, salt (optional)

Instructions:

1. Preheat your oven to 175°C (350°F).

2. Spread peanuts evenly on a baking sheet.

3. Roast peanuts for 10-15 minutes until golden brown and fragrant, stirring occasionally.

4. Allow the roasted peanuts to cool slightly.

5. Transfer the peanuts to your Nutribullet.

6. Add honey and a pinch of salt.

7. Blend until smooth and creamy, scraping down the sides as needed.

8. Transfer the honey roasted peanut butter to a jar or container.

9. Store in the refrigerator for up to 2 weeks.

Nutritional Info: Calories: 220 | Fat: 18g | Carbs: 10g | Protein: 8g

Sunflower Seed Butter

Prep: 10 mins | Cook: 10 mins | Serves: 8

Ingredients:

- US: 500g sunflower seeds, 2 tablespoons coconut oil, salt (optional)

- UK: 500g sunflower seeds, 30ml coconut oil, salt (optional)

Instructions:

1. Toast the sunflower seeds in a dry skillet over medium heat for 5-7 minutes, stirring frequently, until lightly golden and fragrant.

2. Allow the toasted sunflower seeds to cool slightly.

3. Transfer the sunflower seeds to your Nutribullet.

4. Add coconut oil and a pinch of salt.

5. Blend until smooth and creamy, scraping down the sides as needed.

6. Transfer the sunflower seed butter to a jar or container.

7. Store in the refrigerator for up to 2 weeks.

Nutritional Info: Calories: 200 | Fat: 18g | Carbs: 8g | Protein: 7g

Walnut Butter

Prep: 10 mins | Cook: 10 mins | Serves: 8

Ingredients:

- US: 500g walnuts, salt (optional)

- UK: 500g walnuts, salt (optional)

Instructions:

1. Toast the walnuts in a dry skillet over medium heat for 5-7 minutes, stirring frequently, until fragrant and lightly toasted.

2. Allow the toasted walnuts to cool slightly.

3. Transfer the walnuts to your Nutribullet.

4. Blend until smooth and creamy, scraping down the sides as needed.

5. Add salt to taste if desired.

6. Transfer the walnut butter to a jar or container.

7. Store in the refrigerator for up to 2 weeks.

Nutritional Info: Calories: 200 | Fat: 20g | Carbs: 4g | Protein: 5g

CHAPTER 6: FROZEN TREATS

Banana Ice Cream

Prep: 5 mins | Freeze: 4 hours | Serves: 2

Ingredients:

- US: 2 ripe bananas, sliced and frozen
- UK: 2 ripe bananas, sliced and frozen

Instructions:

1. Place the frozen banana slices into your Nutribullet.

2. Blend until smooth, scraping down the sides if necessary.

3. Transfer the creamy mixture into a container and freeze for an additional 1-2 hours to firm up.

4. Scoop into bowls and serve with your favorite toppings.

Strawberry Sorbet

Prep: 10 mins | Freeze: 4 hours | Serves: 2

Ingredients:

- US: 300g strawberries, hulled and halved; 2 tablespoons honey
- UK: 300g strawberries, hulled and halved; 30ml honey

Instructions:

1. In your Nutribullet, blend the strawberries and honey until smooth.

2. Pour the mixture into popsicle molds.

3. Insert popsicle sticks and freeze for at least 4 hours or until set.

4. Remove from molds and enjoy these refreshing treats.

Tropical Fruit Popsicles

Prep: 15 mins | Freeze: 4 hours | Serves: 6

Ingredients:

- US: 2 cups mixed tropical fruits (pineapple, mango, kiwi), chopped; 1 cup coconut water; 3 tablespoons honey

- UK: 450g mixed tropical fruits (pineapple, mango, kiwi), chopped; 240ml coconut water; 45ml honey

Instructions:

1. Combine the mixed tropical fruits, coconut water, and honey in the Nutribullet.

2. Blend until smooth.

3. Pour the mixture into popsicle molds.

4. Insert sticks and freeze for at least 4 hours until solid.

5. Run molds under warm water to release popsicles.

Chocolate Avocado Mousse

Prep: 10 mins | Chill: 1 hour | Serves: 4

Ingredients:

- US: 2 ripe avocados, peeled and pitted; 4 tablespoons cocoa powder; 6 tablespoons maple syrup; 1 teaspoon vanilla extract; pinch of salt

- UK: 2 ripe avocados, peeled and pitted; 60g cocoa powder; 90ml maple syrup; 5ml vanilla extract; pinch of salt

Instructions:

1. Combine all ingredients in the Nutribullet.

2. Blend until smooth and creamy.

3. Chill in the refrigerator for at least 1 hour before serving.

4. Serve chilled, garnished with fresh berries if desired.

Mango Lassi Popsicles

Prep: 10 mins | Freeze: 4 hours | Serves: 6

Ingredients:

- US: 2 ripe mangoes, peeled and diced; 1 cup Greek yogurt; 2 tablespoons honey; 1 teaspoon ground cardamom

- UK: 2 ripe mangoes, peeled and diced; 240ml Greek yogurt; 30ml honey; 5ml ground cardamom

Instructions:

1. Place mangoes, yogurt, honey, and cardamom in the Nutribullet.

2. Blend until smooth.

3. Pour into popsicle molds.

4. Insert sticks and freeze for at least 4 hours until firm.

5. Unmold and enjoy these creamy and fruity popsicles.

Blueberry Coconut Ice Cream

Prep: 5 mins | Freeze: 4 hours | Serves: 2

Ingredients:

- US: 1 cup frozen blueberries; 1 cup coconut milk; 2 tablespoons honey; 1 teaspoon vanilla extract

- UK: 150g frozen blueberries; 240ml coconut milk; 30ml honey; 5ml vanilla extract

Instructions:

1. Combine all ingredients in the Nutribullet.

2. Blend until smooth.

3. Pour the mixture into a shallow container and freeze for 4 hours.

4. Once frozen, scoop and serve as desired.

Green Tea Matcha Ice Cream

Prep: 10 mins | Freeze: 4 hours | Serves: 4

Ingredients:

- US: 2 cups coconut milk; 2 tablespoons matcha powder; 1/2 cup honey; 1 teaspoon vanilla extract

- UK: 480ml coconut milk; 30g matcha powder; 120ml honey; 5ml vanilla extract

Instructions:

1. In the Nutribullet, blend coconut milk, matcha powder, honey, and vanilla extract until smooth.

2. Pour the mixture into a freezer-safe container and freeze for at least 4 hours.

3. Scoop and serve, garnished with additional matcha powder if desired.

Raspberry Lemonade Slushie

Prep: 5 mins | Serves: 2

Ingredients:

- US: 1 cup frozen raspberries; 1 cup lemonade; 1

- UK: 150g frozen raspberries; 240ml lemonade; 1 lemon, juiced; 1 tablespoon honey

Instructions:

1. In the Nutribullet, combine the frozen raspberries, lemonade, lemon juice, and honey.

2. Blend until smooth and slushy.

3. Pour into glasses and serve immediately for a refreshing summer treat.

Peanut Butter Fudge Pops

Prep: 10 mins | Freeze: 4 hours | Serves: 6

Ingredients:

- US: 1/2 cup creamy peanut butter; 2 cups chocolate milk; 1/4 cup cocoa powder; 1/4 cup honey
- UK: 120g creamy peanut butter; 480ml chocolate milk; 30g cocoa powder; 60ml honey

Instructions:

1. Combine peanut butter, chocolate milk, cocoa powder, and honey in the Nutribullet.
2. Blend until smooth.
3. Pour the mixture into popsicle molds.
4. Insert sticks and freeze for at least 4 hours until firm.
5. Enjoy these indulgent peanut butter fudge pops as a delightful frozen treat.

Coconut Lime Granita

Prep: 5 mins | Freeze: 4 hours | Serves: 4

Ingredients:

- US: 2 cups coconut water; 1/2 cup lime juice; 1/4 cup honey; zest of 1 lime
- UK: 480ml coconut water; 120ml lime juice; 60ml honey; zest of 1 lime

Instructions:

1. In a bowl, mix together coconut water, lime juice, honey, and lime zest until well combined.
2. Pour the mixture into a shallow dish or pan.
3. Place in the freezer for about 30 minutes, then scrape with a fork to break up any ice crystals.
4. Repeat scraping every 30 minutes for about 3-4 hours, until the mixture resembles fluffy shaved ice.
5. Serve the coconut lime granita immediately in chilled glasses for a light and refreshing dessert.

CHAPTER 7: JUICES AND TONICS

Green Juice

Prep: 10 mins | Serves: 1

Ingredients:

- US: 1 cup spinach leaves, 1 cucumber (peeled and chopped), 1 green apple (cored and chopped), 1 celery stalk (chopped), 1/2 lemon (juiced), 1/2 cup water

- UK: 100g spinach leaves, 1 cucumber (peeled and chopped), 1 green apple (cored and chopped), 1 celery stalk (chopped), 1/2 lemon (juiced), 120ml water

Instructions:

1. Add spinach, cucumber, apple, celery, lemon juice, and water to the Nutribullet.

2. Blend until smooth.

3. Pour into a glass and serve immediately for a refreshing boost of nutrients.

Beet and Ginger Tonic

Prep: 10 mins | Serves: 1

Ingredients:

- US: 1 small beet (peeled and chopped), 1-inch piece of ginger (peeled and chopped), 1 apple (cored and chopped), 1/2 lemon (juiced), 1 cup water

- UK: 100g small beet (peeled and chopped), 2.5cm piece of ginger (peeled and chopped), 1 apple (cored and chopped), 1/2 lemon (juiced), 240ml water

Instructions:

1. Combine beet, ginger, apple, lemon juice, and water in the Nutribullet.

2. Blend until well combined and smooth.

3. Pour into a glass and enjoy this vibrant and invigorating tonic.

Citrus Refresher

Prep: 5 mins | Serves: 1

Ingredients:

- US: 1 orange (peeled and segmented), 1/2 grapefruit (peeled and segmented), 1/2 lemon (peeled), 1/2 lime (peeled), 1/2 cup coconut water, ice cubes

- UK: 1 orange (peeled and segmented), 1/2 grapefruit (peeled and segmented), 1/2 lemon (peeled), 1/2 lime (peeled), 120ml coconut water, ice cubes

Instructions:

1. Place orange segments, grapefruit segments, lemon, lime, and coconut water into the Nutribullet.

2. Blend until smooth.

3. Add ice cubes and blend again until desired consistency is reached.

4. Pour into a glass and serve immediately for a refreshing citrus pick-me-up.

Carrot and Turmeric Elixir

Prep: 5 mins | Serves: 1

Ingredients:

- US: 1 large carrot (peeled and chopped), 1-inch piece of fresh turmeric (peeled), 1 orange (peeled and segmented), 1/2 lemon (juiced), 1/2 cup coconut water, pinch of black pepper

- UK: 100g large carrot (peeled and chopped), 2.5cm piece of fresh turmeric (peeled), 1 orange (peeled and segmented), 1/2 lemon (juiced), 120ml coconut water, pinch of black pepper

Instructions:

1. Add carrot, turmeric, orange segments, lemon juice, coconut water, and black pepper to the Nutribullet.

2. Blend until smooth and creamy.

3. Pour into a glass and enjoy this vibrant elixir packed with immune-boosting goodness.

Watermelon Mint Refresher

Prep: 5 mins | Serves: 1

Ingredients:

- US: 2 cups diced watermelon, 5-6 fresh mint leaves, 1/2 lime (juiced), 1/2 cup coconut water, ice cubes

- UK: 360g diced watermelon, 5-6 fresh mint leaves, 1/2 lime (juiced), 120ml coconut water, ice cubes

Instructions:

1. Place diced watermelon, mint leaves, lime juice, and coconut water into the Nutribullet.

2. Blend until smooth.

3. Add ice cubes and blend again until well combined.

4. Pour into a glass, garnish with mint leaves, and enjoy this hydrating and refreshing refresher.

Apple Ginger Zinger

Prep: 5 mins | Serves: 1

Ingredients:

- US: 1 apple (cored and chopped), 1-inch piece of ginger (peeled and chopped), 1/2 lemon (juiced), 1/2 cup apple juice, 1/2 cup water

- UK: 1 apple (cored and chopped), 2.5cm piece of ginger (peeled and chopped), 1/2 lemon (juiced), 120ml apple juice, 120ml water

Instructions:

1. Combine chopped apple, ginger, lemon juice, apple juice, and water in the Nutribullet.

2. Blend until smooth and frothy.

3. Pour into a glass and savor the zesty goodness of this apple ginger zinger.

Pineapple Kale Kickstart

Prep: 5 mins | Serves: 1

Ingredients:

- US: 1 cup chopped pineapple, 1 cup kale leaves (stems removed), 1/2 cucumber (peeled and chopped), 1/2 lemon (juiced), 1/2 cup coconut water, ice cubes

- UK: 240g chopped pineapple, 240g kale leaves (stems removed), 1/2 cucumber (peeled and chopped), 1/2 lemon (juiced), 120ml coconut water, ice cubes

Instructions:

1. Add chopped pineapple, kale leaves, cucumber, lemon juice, coconut water, and ice cubes to the Nutribullet.

2. Blend until smooth and creamy.

3. Pour into a glass and kickstart your day with this nutritious and refreshing pineapple kale kickstart.

Berry Beet Blast

Prep: 5 mins | Serves: 1

Ingredients:

- US: 1/2 cup mixed berries (straw berry, blueberry, raspberry), 1 small beet (peeled and chopped), 1/2 banana (sliced), 1/2 cup almond milk, 1 tablespoon honey or maple syrup (optional)

- UK: 60g mixed berries (strawberry, blueberry, raspberry), 100g small beet (peeled and chopped), 1/2 banana (sliced), 120ml almond milk, 15ml honey or maple syrup (optional)

Instructions:

1. Place mixed berries, chopped beet, sliced banana, almond milk, and honey or maple syrup (if using) into the Nutribullet.

2. Blend until smooth and creamy.

3. Pour into a glass and enjoy this vibrant berry beet blast packed with antioxidants and vitamins.

Cucumber Melon Cooler

Prep: 5 mins | Serves: 1

Ingredients:

- US: 1/2 cucumber (peeled and chopped), 1 cup diced honeydew melon, 1/2 lime (juiced), 1/4 cup fresh mint leaves, 1/2 cup coconut water, ice cubes

- UK: 1/2 cucumber (peeled and chopped), 240g diced honeydew melon, 1/2 lime (juiced), 15g fresh mint leaves, 120ml coconut water, ice cubes

Instructions:

1. Add chopped cucumber, diced honeydew melon, lime juice, fresh mint leaves, coconut water, and ice cubes to the Nutribullet.

2. Blend until well combined and smooth.

3. Pour into a glass, garnish with a mint sprig, and enjoy this refreshing cucumber melon cooler.

Pomegranate Chia Fresca

Prep: 5 mins (+ 30 mins soaking time for chia seeds) | Serves: 1

Ingredients:

- US: 1/2 cup pomegranate juice, 1/2 cup coconut water, 1 tablespoon chia seeds, 1/2 lime (juiced), honey or maple syrup to taste (optional)

- UK: 120ml pomegranate juice, 120ml coconut water, 15g chia seeds, 1/2 lime (juiced), honey or maple syrup to taste (optional)

Instructions:

1. In a small bowl, mix pomegranate juice and coconut water.

2. Add chia seeds and lime juice, and stir well.

3. Let the mixture sit for about 30 minutes to allow the chia seeds to plump up.

4. Pour into a glass, sweeten with honey or maple syrup if desired, and enjoy this hydrating and nutrient-rich pomegranate chia fresca.

CHAPTER 8: BABY AND TODDLER PUREES

Sweet Potato and Apple Baby Puree

Prep: 10 mins | Cook: 15 mins | Serves: 4

Ingredients:

- US: 300g sweet potato (peeled and diced), 200g apple (peeled, cored, and diced), water

- UK: 300g sweet potato (peeled and diced), 200g apple (peeled, cored, and diced), water

Instructions:

1. Steam the sweet potato and apple until tender, about 10-15 minutes.

2. Transfer the steamed sweet potato and apple to the Nutribullet.

3. Add a little water to achieve the desired consistency.

4. Blend until smooth and creamy.

5. Serve the sweet potato and apple puree warm or chilled.

Broccoli and Cheddar Toddler Puree

Prep: 10 mins | Cook: 15 mins | Serves: 4

Ingredients:

- US: 300g broccoli florets, 50g cheddar cheese (grated), water

- UK: 300g broccoli florets, 50g cheddar cheese (grated), water

Instructions:

1. Steam the broccoli florets until tender, about 10-15 minutes.

2. Transfer the steamed broccoli to the Nutribullet.

3. Add grated cheddar cheese to the broccoli.

4. Blend until smooth, adding water as needed for desired consistency.

5. Serve the broccoli and cheddar puree warm.

Banana and Blueberry Baby Puree

Prep: 5 mins | Serves: 4

Ingredients:

- US: 2 ripe bananas, 150g blueberries, water

- UK: 2 ripe bananas, 150g blueberries, water

Instructions:

1. Peel the bananas and place them in the Nutribullet.

2. Add the blueberries to the bananas.

3. Blend until smooth, adding water as needed to reach the desired consistency.

4. Serve the banana and blueberry puree chilled.

Spinach and Pear Baby Puree

Prep: 10 mins | Cook: 5 mins | Serves: 4

Ingredients:

- US: 200g spinach leaves, 2 ripe pears (peeled, cored, and diced), water

- UK: 200g spinach leaves, 2 ripe pears (peeled, cored, and diced), water

Instructions:

1. Steam the spinach leaves until wilted, about 5 minutes.

2. Transfer the steamed spinach and diced pears to the Nutribullet.

3. Blend until smooth, adding water as needed for desired consistency.

4. Serve the spinach and pear puree warm or chilled.

Butternut Squash and Carrot Baby Puree

Prep: 10 mins | Cook: 15 mins | Serves: 4

Ingredients:

- US: 300g butternut squash (peeled and diced), 200g carrots (peeled and diced), water

- UK: 300g butternut squash (peeled and diced), 200g carrots (peeled and diced), water

Instructions:

1. Steam the butternut squash and carrots until tender, about 10-15 minutes.

2. Transfer the steamed vegetables to the Nutribullet.

3. Blend until smooth, adding water as needed to achieve desired consistency.

4. Serve the butternut squash and carrot puree warm.

Peach and Oatmeal Baby Puree

Prep: 5 mins | Cook: 10 mins | Serves: 4

Ingredients:

- US: 2 ripe peaches (peeled, pitted, and diced), 50g rolled oats, water

- UK: 2 ripe peaches (peeled, pitted, and diced), 50g rolled oats, water

Instructions:

1. In a saucepan, combine diced peaches, rolled oats, and enough water to cover.

2. Cook over medium heat until peaches are soft and oats are cooked, about 10 minutes.

3. Transfer the cooked mixture to the Nutribullet.

4. Blend until smooth, adding more water if needed for desired consistency.

5. Serve the peach and oatmeal puree warm.

Green Bean and Potato Toddler Puree

Prep: 10 mins | Cook: 15 mins | Serves: 4

Ingredients:

- US: 300g green beans (trimmed and chopped), 200g potatoes (peeled and diced), water
- UK: 300g green beans (trimmed and chopped), 200g potatoes (peeled and diced), water

Instructions:

1. Steam the green beans and diced potatoes until tender, about 10-15 minutes.
2. Transfer the steamed vegetables to the Nutribullet.
3. Blend until smooth, adding water as needed for desired consistency.
4. Serve the green bean and potato puree warm.

Mango and Yogurt Baby Puree

Prep: 5 mins | Serves: 4

Ingredients:

- US: 2 ripe mangoes (peeled, pitted, and diced), 150g plain yogurt
- UK: 2 ripe mangoes (peeled, pitted, and diced), 150g plain yogurt

Instructions:

1. Place diced mangoes and yogurt in the Nutribullet.
2. Blend until smooth and creamy.
3. Serve the mango and yogurt puree chilled.

Avocado and Kiwi Baby Puree

Prep: 5 mins | Serves: 4

Ingredients:

- US: 2 ripe avocados (peeled and pitted), 2 ripe kiwis (peeled and diced)

- UK: 2 ripe avocados (peeled and pitted), 2 ripe kiwis (peeled and diced)

Instructions:

1. Place avocados and diced kiwis in the Nutribullet.

2. Blend until smooth and creamy.

3. Serve the avocado and kiwi puree chilled.

Zucchini and Lentil Baby Puree

Prep: 10 mins | Cook: 20 mins | Serves: 4

Ingredients:

- US: 300g zucchini (peeled and diced), 100g dried red lentils, water

- UK: 300g zucchini (peeled and diced), 100g dried red lentils, water

Instructions:

1. Cook red lentils according to package instructions until tender, about 15-20 minutes.

2. Steam the diced zucchini until soft, about 5-7 minutes.

3. Transfer the cooked lentils and zucchini to the Nutribullet.

4. Blend until smooth, adding water if needed for desired consistency.

5. Serve the zucchini and lentil puree warm.

CHAPTER 9: BOOSTERS AND SUPERFOODS

Protein Powder Blends

Prep: 5 mins | Serves: 1

Ingredients:

- US: 1 scoop protein powder, 1 banana, 250ml almond milk, handful of spinach
- UK: 1 scoop protein powder, 1 banana, 250ml almond milk, handful of spinach

Instructions:

1. Add all ingredients to the Nutribullet cup.
2. Blend until smooth and creamy.
3. Enjoy this protein-packed smoothie as a post-workout refuel.

Chia Seed Pudding

Prep: 5 mins (+2 hours chilling) | Serves: 2

Ingredients:

- US: 60g chia seeds, 250ml almond milk, 1 tablespoon maple syrup, 1/2 teaspoon vanilla extract
- UK: 60g chia seeds, 250ml almond milk, 1 tablespoon maple syrup, 1/2 teaspoon vanilla extract

Instructions:

1. In a bowl, mix chia seeds, almond milk, maple syrup, and vanilla extract.
2. Let it sit for 5 minutes, then whisk again.
3. Refrigerate for at least 2 hours or overnight until thickened.
4. Serve chilled with your favorite toppings.

Acai Bowl

Prep: 10 mins | Serves: 1

Ingredients:

- US: 1 packet frozen acai, 1/2 banana, 100g mixed berries, 50ml almond milk, toppings of choice (granola, sliced fruits, nuts, seeds)

- UK: 1 packet frozen acai, 1/2 banana, 100g mixed berries, 50ml almond milk, toppings of choice (granola, sliced fruits, nuts, seeds)

Instructions:

1. Blend acai, banana, mixed berries, and almond milk until smooth.

2. Pour into a bowl and add desired toppings.

3. Enjoy this nutritious and delicious acai bowl for breakfast or as a refreshing snack.

Turmeric Latte

Prep: 5 mins | Cook: 5 mins | Serves: 2

Ingredients:

- US: 500ml almond milk, 1 tablespoon honey, 1 teaspoon ground turmeric, 1/2 teaspoon ground cinnamon, 1/4 teaspoon ground ginger, pinch of black pepper

- UK: 500ml almond milk, 1 tablespoon honey, 1 teaspoon ground turmeric, 1/2 teaspoon ground cinnamon, 1/4 teaspoon ground ginger, pinch of black pepper

Instructions:

1. In a saucepan, heat almond milk, honey, turmeric, cinnamon, ginger, and black pepper.

2. Whisk until hot but not boiling.

3. Pour into mugs and serve warm.

Matcha Green Tea Smoothie

Prep: 5 mins | Serves: 1

Ingredients:

- US: 1 teaspoon matcha powder, 1 banana, 100ml coconut milk, 50g spinach, 1 tablespoon honey

- UK: 1 teaspoon matcha powder, 1 banana, 100ml coconut milk, 50g spinach, 1 tablespoon honey

Instructions:

1. Blend matcha powder, banana, coconut milk, spinach, and honey until smooth.

2. Pour into a glass and enjoy this energizing green smoothie.

Spirulina Smoothie

Prep: 5 mins | Serves: 1

Ingredients:

- US: 1 teaspoon spirulina powder, 1/2 cup pineapple chunks, 1/2 cup mango chunks, 100ml coconut water, handful of kale

- UK: 1 teaspoon spirulina powder, 1/2 cup pineapple chunks, 1/2 cup mango chunks, 100ml coconut water, handful of kale

Instructions:

1. Combine spirulina powder, pineapple chunks, mango chunks, coconut water, and kale in the Nutribullet.

2. Blend until smooth and enjoy this nutrient-rich smoothie.

Maca Root Energy Balls

Prep: 15 mins | Chill: 30 mins | Makes: 12 balls

Ingredients:

- US: 1 cup rolled oats, 1/2 cup almond butter, 1/4 cup honey, 2 tablespoons maca powder, 1/4 cup chopped almonds, 1/4 cup shredded coconut

- UK: 1 cup rolled oats, 1/2 cup almond butter, 1/4 cup honey, 2 tablespoons maca powder, 1/4 cup chopped almonds, 1/4 cup shredded coconut

Instructions:

1. In a bowl, mix rolled oats, almond butter, honey, maca powder, chopped almonds, and shredded coconut.

2. Roll the mixture into balls and place on a baking sheet.

3. Chill in the fridge for 30 minutes before serving.

Goji Berry Granola

Prep: 10 mins | Cook: 25 mins | Serves: 6

Ingredients:

- US: 2 cups rolled oats, 1/4 cup maple syrup, 2 tablespoons coconut oil, 1/2 cup goji berries, 1/4 cup chopped almonds, 1/4 cup pumpkin seeds

- UK: 2 cups rolled oats, 1/4 cup maple syrup, 2 tablespoons coconut oil, 1/2 cup goji berries, 1/4 cup chopped almonds, 1/4 cup pumpkin seeds

Instructions:

1. Preheat the oven to 160°C (325°F) and line a baking sheet with parchment paper.

2. In a bowl, mix rolled oats, maple syrup, coconut oil, goji berries, chopped almonds, and pumpkin seeds.

3. Spread the mixture evenly on the baking sheet and bake for 25 minutes, stirring halfway through.

4. Let cool completely before storing in an airtight container.

Cacao Nibs Trail Mix

Prep: 5 mins | Serves: 4

Ingredients:

- US: 1/2 cup almonds, 1/2 cup cashews, 1/4 cup cacao nibs, 1/4 cup dried cranberries, 1/4 cup pumpkin seeds

- UK: 1/2 cup almonds, 1/2 cup cashews, 1/4 cup cacao nibs, 1/4 cup dried cranberries, 1/4 cup pumpkin seeds

Instructions:

1. In a bowl, combine almonds, cashews, cacao nibs, dried cranberries, and pumpkin seeds.

2. Mix well and store in an airtight container for a convenient and nutritious snack.

Flaxseed Crackers

Prep: 10 mins | Cook: 25 mins | Serves: 4

Ingredients:

- US: 1 cup ground flaxseeds, 1/4 cup water, 1/2 teaspoon garlic powder, 1/2 teaspoon onion powder, 1/4 teaspoon sea salt, 1 tablespoon sesame seeds

- UK: 1 cup ground flaxseeds, 1/4 cup water, 1/2 teaspoon garlic powder, 1/2 teaspoon onion powder, 1/4 teaspoon sea salt, 1 tablespoon sesame seeds

Instructions:

1. Preheat the oven to 175°C (350°F) and line a baking sheet with parchment paper.

2. In a bowl, mix ground flaxseeds, water, garlic powder, onion powder, and sea salt until a dough forms.

3. Place the dough between two sheets of parchment paper and roll out thinly.

4. Remove the top layer of parchment paper and sprinkle sesame seeds over the dough.

5. Using a pizza cutter or knife, score the dough into desired cracker shapes.

6. Bake for 20-25 minutes until golden and crisp.

7. Allow to cool completely before breaking into crackers.

CHAPTER 10: SAVORY SNACKS AND SIDES

Zucchini Fritters

Prep: 15 mins | Cook: 15 mins | Serves: 4

Ingredients:

- US: 2 medium zucchinis, grated and squeezed dry, 1/4 cup all-purpose flour, 1/4 cup grated Parmesan cheese, 1 egg, lightly beaten, 2 cloves garlic, minced, 2 tablespoons chopped fresh parsley, salt, pepper, olive oil (for frying)

- UK: 2 medium courgettes, grated and squeezed dry, 30g all-purpose flour, 30g grated Parmesan cheese, 1 egg, lightly beaten, 2 cloves garlic, minced, 2 tablespoons chopped fresh parsley, salt, pepper, olive oil (for frying)

Instructions:

1. In a large bowl, combine grated zucchini, flour, Parmesan cheese, egg, garlic, parsley, salt, and pepper.

2. Heat olive oil in a non-stick skillet over medium heat.

3. Scoop about 2 tablespoons of the zucchini mixture and flatten it into a pancake shape.

4. Place the fritters in the skillet and cook for 3-4 minutes on each side until golden brown and crispy.

5. Remove from the skillet and place on a paper towel-lined plate to drain excess oil.

6. Repeat with the remaining zucchini mixture.

7. Serve the zucchini fritters hot with your favorite dipping sauce.

Cauliflower Tots

Prep: 20 mins | Cook: 25 mins | Serves: 4

Ingredients:

- US: 1 small head cauliflower, cut into florets, 1/4 cup grated Parmesan cheese, 1/4 cup breadcrumbs, 1 egg, lightly beaten, 2 tablespoons chopped fresh chives, salt, pepper, cooking spray

- UK: 1 small head cauliflower, cut into florets, 30g grated Parmesan cheese, 30g breadcrumbs, 1 egg, lightly beaten, 2 tablespoons chopped fresh chives, salt, pepper, cooking spray

Instructions:

1. Preheat the oven to 200°C (400°F) and line a baking sheet with parchment paper.

2. Steam the cauliflower florets until tender, about 8-10 minutes. Allow to cool slightly.

3. In a large bowl, mash the steamed cauliflower with a fork or potato masher.

4. Add Parmesan cheese, breadcrumbs, egg, chives, salt, and pepper to the mashed cauliflower and mix until well combined.

5. Shape the mixture into small tots and place them on the prepared baking sheet.

6. Lightly spray the tots with cooking spray.

7. Bake in the preheated oven for 15-20 minutes until golden and crispy.

8. Serve the cauliflower tots hot with ketchup or your favorite dipping sauce.

Beet Hummus

Prep: 15 mins | Cook: 0 mins | Serves: 4

Ingredients:

- US: 1 can (400g) chickpeas, drained and rinsed, 2 medium beets, cooked and peeled, 3 tablespoons tahini, 2 cloves garlic, minced, 3 tablespoons lemon juice, 2 tablespoons olive oil, 1/2 teaspoon ground cumin, salt, pepper

- UK: 1 can (400g) chickpeas, drained and rinsed, 2 medium beets, cooked and peeled, 3 tablespoons tahini, 2 cloves garlic, minced, 3 tablespoons lemon juice, 2 tablespoons olive oil, 1/2 teaspoon ground cumin, salt, pepper

Instructions:

1. In a Nutribullet or food processor, combine chickpeas, cooked beets, tahini, garlic, lemon juice, olive oil, cumin, salt, and pepper.

2. Blend until smooth and creamy, scraping down the sides as needed.

3. If the hummus is too thick, add a little water to reach the desired consistency.

4. Taste and adjust seasoning if needed.

5. Transfer the beet hummus to a serving bowl and drizzle with olive oil.

6. Serve with pita bread, vegetable sticks, or crackers.

Edamame Guacamole

Prep: 10 mins | Cook: 0 mins | Serves: 4

Ingredients:

- US: 1 cup shelled edamame, thawed if frozen, 2 ripe avocados, peeled and pitted, 1/4 cup chopped red onion, 1/4 cup chopped fresh cilantro, 1 jalapeno, seeded and minced, 2 tablespoons lime juice, 1 clove garlic, minced, salt, pepper

- UK: 150g shelled edamame, thawed if frozen, 2 ripe avocados, peeled and pitted, 30g chopped red onion, 30g chopped fresh coriander, 1 jalapeno, seeded and minced, 2 tablespoons lime juice, 1 clove garlic, minced, salt, pepper

Instructions:

1. In a Nutribullet or food processor, combine shelled edamame, avocados, red onion, cilantro, jalapeno, lime juice, garlic, salt, and pepper.

2. Pulse until the ingredients are well combined but still slightly chunky.

3. Taste and adjust seasoning if needed.

4. Transfer the edamame guacamole to a serving bowl.

5. Serve with tortilla chips or as a topping for tacos and burrito bowls.

Carrot and Parsnip Fries

Prep: 10 mins | Cook: 25 mins | Serves: 4

Ingredients:

- US: 2 large carrots, peeled and cut into sticks, 2 large parsnips, peeled and cut into sticks, 2 tablespoons olive oil, 1 teaspoon paprika, 1/2 teaspoon garlic powder, 1/2 teaspoon onion powder, salt, pepper

- UK: 2 large carrots, peeled and cut into sticks, 2 large parsnips, peeled and cut into sticks, 2 tablespoons olive oil, 1 teaspoon paprika, 1/2 teaspoon garlic powder, 1/2 teaspoon onion powder, salt, pepper

Instructions:

1. Preheat your oven to 220°C (425°F) and line a baking sheet with parchment paper.

2. In a large bowl, toss together the carrot and parsnip sticks with olive oil, paprika, garlic powder, onion powder, salt, and pepper until evenly coated.

3. Spread the seasoned carrot and parsnip sticks in a single layer on the prepared baking sheet.

4. Bake in the preheated oven for 20-25 minutes, flipping halfway through, until the fries are golden brown and crispy.

5. Once cooked, remove from the oven and serve immediately.

6. Enjoy these delicious carrot and parsnip fries as a healthier alternative to traditional fries!

Sweet Potato Falafels

Prep: 20 mins | Cook: 25 mins | Serves: 4

Ingredients:

- US: 2 cups cooked sweet potatoes, mashed, 1 can (400g) chickpeas, drained and rinsed, 1/4 cup chopped fresh parsley, 2 cloves garlic, minced, 1 teaspoon ground cumin, 1 teaspoon ground coriander, 1/4 teaspoon cayenne pepper, 2 tablespoons chickpea flour, salt, pepper, olive oil (for frying)

- UK: 400g cooked sweet potatoes, mashed, 1 can (400g) chickpeas, drained and rinsed, 30g chopped fresh parsley, 2 cloves garlic, minced, 1 teaspoon ground cumin, 1 teaspoon ground coriander, 1/4 teaspoon cayenne pepper, 2 tablespoons chickpea flour, salt, pepper, olive oil (for frying)

Instructions:

1. In a Nutribullet or food processor, combine mashed sweet potatoes, chickpeas, parsley, garlic, cumin, coriander, cayenne pepper, chickpea flour, salt, and pepper.

2. Pulse until the mixture comes together but is still slightly chunky.

3. Shape the mixture into small patties or balls.

4. Heat olive oil in a non-stick skillet over medium heat.

5. Cook the sweet potato falafels for 3-4 minutes on each side until golden brown and crispy.

6. Once cooked, transfer to a paper towel-lined plate to drain excess oil.

7. Serve the sweet potato falafels warm with tahini sauce or yogurt dip.

Kale Chips

Prep: 10 mins | Cook: 20 mins | Serves: 4

Ingredients:

- US: 1 bunch kale, stems removed and torn into bite-sized pieces, 2 tablespoons olive oil, 1 tablespoon nutritional yeast, 1/2 teaspoon garlic powder, 1/2 teaspoon onion powder, salt, pepper

- UK: 1 bunch kale, stems removed and torn into bite-sized pieces, 30ml olive oil, 15g nutritional yeast, 1/2 teaspoon garlic powder, 1/2 teaspoon onion powder, salt, pepper

Instructions:

1. Preheat your oven to 150°C (300°F) and line a baking sheet with parchment paper.

2. In a large bowl, massage the kale pieces with olive oil until well coated.

3. Sprinkle nutritional yeast, garlic powder, onion powder, salt, and pepper over the kale and toss to combine.

4. Spread the kale in a single layer on the prepared baking sheet.

5. Bake in the preheated oven for 15-20 minutes, until the kale is crispy but not burnt.

6. Remove from the oven and let cool slightly before serving.

7. Enjoy these crunchy kale chips as a healthy snack or side dish!

Black Bean Brownies

Prep: 15 mins | Cook: 25 mins | Serves: 9

Ingredients:

- US: 1 can (400g) black beans, drained and rinsed, 3 large eggs, 1/4 cup cocoa powder, 1/2 cup maple syrup, 1/4 cup coconut oil, melted, 1 teaspoon vanilla extract, 1/2 teaspoon baking powder, 1/4 teaspoon salt, 1/2 cup chocolate chips

- UK: 1 can (400g) black beans, drained and rinsed, 3 large eggs, 30g cocoa powder, 120ml maple syrup, 60ml coconut oil, melted, 5ml vanilla extract, 2.5ml baking powder, 1.25ml salt, 70g chocolate chips

Instructions:

1. Preheat your oven to 180°C (350°F) and grease an 8x8-inch baking dish.

2. In a Nutribullet or food processor, blend black beans, eggs, cocoa powder, maple syrup, coconut oil, vanilla extract, baking powder, and salt until smooth.

3. Stir in chocolate chips until evenly distributed.

4. Pour the batter into the prepared baking dish and spread it out evenly.

5. Bake in the preheated oven for 20-25 minutes, or until the brownies are set and a toothpick inserted into the center comes out clean.

6. Allow the brownies to cool completely before slicing and serving.

7. Enjoy these decadent black bean brownies guilt-free!

Broccoli Tots

Prep: 20 mins | Cook: 25 mins | Serves: 4

Ingredients:

- US: 2 cups finely chopped broccoli florets, 1 cup breadcrumbs, 1/2 cup shredded cheddar cheese, 1/4 cup grated Parmesan cheese, 1 large egg, lightly beaten, 2 cloves garlic, minced, 2 tablespoons chopped fresh parsley, salt, pepper, cooking spray

- UK: 150g finely chopped broccoli florets, 60g breadcrumbs, 60g shredded cheddar cheese, 30g grated Parmesan cheese, 1 large egg, lightly beaten, 2 cloves garlic, minced, 2 tablespoons chopped fresh parsley, salt, pepper, cooking spray

Instructions:

1. Preheat your oven to 200°C (400°F) and line a baking sheet with parchment paper.

2. In a large bowl, combine chopped broccoli, breadcrumbs, cheddar cheese, Parmesan cheese, egg, garlic, parsley, salt, and pepper.

3. Mix until well combined and the mixture holds together when squeezed.

4. Shape the mixture into small tots and place them on the prepared baking sheet.

5. Lightly spray the tots with cooking spray.

6. Bake in the preheated oven for 20-25 minutes, flipping halfway through, until golden and crispy.

7. Serve the broccoli tots hot with your favorite dipping sauce.

Roasted Chickpeas

Prep: 10 mins |Cook: 35 mins | Serves: 4

Ingredients:

- US: 2 cans (400g each) chickpeas, drained, rinsed, and patted dry, 2 tablespoons olive oil, 1 teaspoon ground cumin, 1 teaspoon paprika, 1/2 teaspoon garlic powder, 1/2 teaspoon onion powder, salt, pepper

- UK: 2 cans (400g each) chickpeas, drained, rinsed, and patted dry, 30ml olive oil, 5g ground cumin, 5g paprika, 2.5g garlic powder, 2.5g onion powder, salt, pepper

Instructions:

1. Preheat your oven to 200°C (400°F) and line a baking sheet with parchment paper.

2. In a large bowl, toss the chickpeas with olive oil, ground cumin, paprika, garlic powder, onion powder, salt, and pepper until evenly coated.

3. Spread the seasoned chickpeas in a single layer on the prepared baking sheet.

4. Bake in the preheated oven for 30-35 minutes, shaking the pan occasionally, until the chickpeas are crispy and golden brown.

5. Remove from the oven and let cool slightly before serving.

6. Enjoy these roasted chickpeas as a crunchy and flavorful snack!

CONCLUSION

As I look back on my journey from NutriBullet skeptic to superfan, I'm filled with immense gratitude for this powerful little blender and how it transformed my relationship with food. What started as a desperate attempt to lose weight quickly evolved into a passion for nurturing my body with delicious, nutrient-dense foods that make me feel amazing from the inside out.

In these pages, I've shared hundreds of sweet and savory NutriBullet creations that I've carefully developed and tested in my own kitchen. From thick, indulgent smoothie bowls to replace dessert cravings, to light, zingy juices perfect for a refreshing pick-me-up, each recipe provides a mega-dose of fruits, veggies, and other wholesome ingredients in outrageously tasty ways.

Creating these blends is an act of self-care, whether you're whipping up a quick breakfast smoothie before heading to work or crafting an involved nut milk or dip for a special occasion. The simple ritual of tossing fresh ingredients into the NutriBullet and experiencing that smooth, creamy blend come together is incredibly satisfying and grounding.

While striving to make nutritious choices is incredibly important, I've also learned that conscious eating shouldn't mean deprivation or feeling stuck with bland, boring meals. Thanks to the NutriBullet's unique extraction abilities, vibrant flavors and decadent textures can be achieved without butter, cream, or refined sugars.

Don't get me wrong - I still enjoy treats on occasion! But now, I get my "dessert" fix from blending up a thick, frosty Pumpkin Pie Shake or Peanut Butter Cup Smoothie Bowl without the guilt. For quick meals, I can easily whip up a hearty, warming soup like the Cream of Tomato or Loaded Baked Potato in the NutriBullet in minutes. Its versatility is simply amazing.

My hope is that this book has not only provided you with an arsenal of inspiring recipes to try, but has also empowered you with the tools and techniques to start experimenting and crafting your own signature NutriBullet blends. Once you get the hang of combining ingredients for craveable flavors and textures, the possibilities are truly endless!

If you've been on the fence about taking the NutriBullet plunge, I encourage you to simply try it for a week. Commit to having at least one nutrient-packed NutriBullet smoothie or shake each day, and I'm confident you'll soon be experiencing a difference in your energy levels, clarity, digestion and overall well-being. It's that powerful.

I'm forever grateful to have rediscovered my love for wholesome, flavorful foods through the NutriBullet. This compact powerhouse has been a key part of my health and weight loss journey, but also so much more. It's helped me see the kitchen as a sanctuary for nurturing my body, rather than a source of struggle or deprivation. I can't wait to see how it will transform your life as well. Here's to balanced nutrition made deliciously simple!

Printed in Great Britain
by Amazon